The Little Red House

THE LITTLE RED HOUSE

The Selected Poems of
LARRY BENJAMIN

Mountain Arbor
  Press
Alpharetta, GA

This is a work of fiction. Names, characters, businesses, places, and events are either the products of the author's imagination or are used in a fictitious manner. Any resemblance to actual persons, living or dead, or actual events is purely coincidental.

Copyright © 2020 by Larry Benjamin

All rights reserved. No part of this book may be reproduced or transmitted in any form or by any means, electronic or mechanical, including photocopying, recording, or any information storage and retrieval system, without permission in writing from the author.

ISBN: 978-1-63183-769-2 - Paperback
eISBN: 978-1-63183-770-8 - ePub
eISBN: 978-1-63183-771-5 - mobi

Library of Congress Control Number: 2020908859

Printed in the United States of America   0 5 1 8 2 0

∞This paper meets the requirements of ANSI/NISO Z39.48-1992 (Permanence of Paper)

For Mary.
Who else?

For Number
38363

And for all
of them.

La parole humaine est comme un chaudron fêlé où nous battons des mélodies à faire danser les ours, quand on voudrait attendrir les étoiles.

—Gustave Flaubert

Contents

A Short Waltz before the Vehmgericht	1
Need Not Worry	22
The Cudgel and the Dragonfly	25
Repetition	29
The Scout	36
Vogel als Prophet	41
An Effort	47
Surface	50
What One Finds in the Clay	54
Next	59
Blocks of Words	62
Little Friend	69
Over the Top	76
A Country like a Diseased Dance	85

A Short Waltz before the Vehmgericht

as the door opens

"Good day."

"And to you, really, and welcome," it says. "This must be unexpected. My appearance, perhaps? Of course not. You chose so often the color of my eyes, the heft of my undulating hand. It so happens that verbs do dart from this side of the defoliated line. I greet you, quiet now, more than you, me."

"You cannot ascertain. What should I do?"

"Not a thing," it says. "There is no doing here and no such thing. Feel enabled, however, to carve those miserable tonal vibrations, perhaps, if you so wish. No difference will come of it. Who could shape whatever encapsulates silence? This is no time to reflect, for here is no time, no mind, and no is. The feeble bricks, nonetheless, are made available. What is your song?"

"It is veritably short, all contained in the ultimate, mottled encounter."

"No affection for we tend to object. See it is funny. But pray narrate," it says.

* * *

There are five of them, their backs to me. Proud companions, but dry and subdued, with unfinished business, they declare to carry other juicy stones. Hence my conviction that they came for the same oblique reason I did; it lasts another heartbeat. Sleek and reddish greaves on, offering more than freedom and so much less than tremor or pain, they peruse rumors bubbling out of the drying mud: "You won't feel a thing," they chant, still boyishly interested. Not feeling a thing? Sounds like a plan. I do not waver or stumble. Come and inject your serene gift.

They do not. Are they as uncomfortable as I am with asymmetrical arrangements?

"We agree or we don't," they murmur with a guffaw. And fall asleep.

A Short Waltz before the Vehmgericht

Later one leaves. That is when she enters and it stops. They have to ignore her. To them, she is the wrathful specter, the filthy wraith. There was

a first

time

for

it

all. Nonetheless it started long ago, before the moon's pigmentation became rightfully reflected, before noon, when her hair was not quite fluttering. Is there a word for it?

Now that is a stupid, stupid question, suggesting paucity of knowledge, lack of imagination. Do not blame it on me.

They operate with curved implements of oak, she with

with

with

You've got it, soldier.

a single eyelash, equally bent. Both suit me. A translation is a translation is a translation. Enough, you catch my drift, reverend reference.

They, forever across the border, must have caught it too.

She fulfills, you understand, no method. The vain master of virtual pebbles whose trinity never added up would blush (is he around?) at her counterexamples. She engages the warmth, the inward manifestation of her senses. Unfortunately, they thrive on heat or, depending, marionberry.

Or strive?

I do not, do not know.

The smallest of the four sidesteps farther away. Another friend to meet, I speculate, of ideal size, not too nimble, not too dumb. She enters and it stops. I cannot pledge whether she walks or glides or hovers or rests. I fear her more than they do for the service they offer holds no startling fume. No doubt

No doubt? Are you certain?

No doubt: Hear ye, hear ye, let it be known. I will receive cinders from them or a tubular dram of liquid coal from any blind peddler solely upon her billowy nod.

Please, this hurts.

Not the whisper of a tearing doubt, you magnificent theorists.

This creature

Oh, she is no simple, what do you call them? Well, she is not, is she? As if there

is an infallible phantom I trust, I trust, here or not here or there or there again. I keep a triangular list, incarnate, translucent, of lexicons to discard, spells to encase, harmonies to bury. For fear of her acquiescing, I grant, I will show it to no one. She might, after all, confront me alone with them or then again would not listen.

The three travelers are staring at me, playing their drums, humming. I have not observed them turning around. "Come closer." Who opened up? The next blink will be no cinch, no piece of cake, no walk in the park, no picnic, no bowl of cherries.

We get it. Repetitions will kill you.

I bat a lid, I die.

Oh, so you said a bad word. Not like you.

But what a jewel.

She enters and it stops without an answer from her. Too busy exhausting all that is possible, she pays no heed to rusty rejoinders. There is no no in her parlance. "Why not confuse the arrow and the scale," she throws, "as both may pierce the tea-colored area? Give them a chance." Her sinuous trajectory in the sandy room bears resemblance to weightless water on heated rock. The lock briefly touches the cheek, then returns to a place akin to hint or shade or wall. You know how much I have warned her warned her warned her: "Draw a likeness of my heart and it will poison you, starting with the eye socket, its floating surface, all the way to fluted, thin-as-Freon hands. May I slumber in the ruination you relinquish?" After the one and only day, I harbor no belief in the staccato of hollow tools.

Nonetheless, she stands and shakes her head in cold rage. She, the antidote in rebuttal of absorption; she, the scorpion tamer

Nasty, minable. So this is what they are? Why did you have to make it appear so complicated? Can't you state things clearly?

Poor

poor

poorest

man's Diderot.

Watch your mouth, private. No analogy or metaphor here: nothing stands for something else. Nothing stands. No linguistics, no phonetics, no pragmatics, no semiotics. Boring, is it not?

Useless and uncertain.

And I was about to forget: no quotations, not a single more.

What can I say? Nothing linear as shards about her, only her steadfast sarissa aimed at wiry universes. But I digress: She, the obverse of my survivors, bears a name which hurts merely the soul, as do her double-edged patience and radiance, from days on earth, around earth, in earth along with rhizome, rust, and nascent bees.

The soul? The soul? Look around, my friend. What are you talking about?

Neither do I accept. Yet she enters

And it stopped?

In tense tense it stops indeed. Her vague alacrity so like a forge, a square, formidable silence falls all over like tepid hail, covering all, smothering doubt

Again? You are not going to last. Of course, here, lasting is

to say nothing of skulls.

Optional. But this is better.

Periodically she fades as well as per desires. That fragment of silver I call my will is contained within her. I shake of it.

The animals (I insist, not beasts), naturally, remain to change the guard. Why would there be no snake? Reptiles proclaim in clear, but instead, these? These are times of the essence, when tables and ties and screens and folios turn from mortar to blood. For she will enter and it will stop, return to the selfsame place or hint or shade or wall.

Rhetorical loop! You are losing momentum.

They have their tactics. I have mine, fitful, so it goes and flows strangely ebbing the same way. You promised I could sing my song, she is in it.

I made no promise. I only asked what the song was. You always jump to conclusions. For instance now.

Hanging Thai silk scorches nothing she cannot emulate. Chestnuts in a Normandy fireplace, dog sound asleep, mares scraped and tethered, will go rampant if she sees fit to sigh. That tower, that alabaster blade, reaches nowhere near her skin.

But I relapse. I refuse as those hunters refused such peremptory leap over the hedge in the morning. Stubbornly she, too, enters and it stops.

What do you have that stops?

A Short Waltz before the Vehmgericht

I tell you, though she has no credence in those things. You do, I do. The crepitation of larks, the buzzing of something that is not quite a fly near the body of the fallen, a short, upside-down prayer I imagined, a beeping emptiness for the ages, the taste of ether on my steel tongue

Borrowed from Homer, I fear. And I specified you couldn't.

when the door was shut one final time, sharp sugars for those who, in a pile, no longer mattering, apply some degree of closure to their laughter.

Description?

We speak words undone. We build epic laws unsaid. She looks at me and I crumble, avert my comatose eyes, perceive the dust turning into foundation.

This is mediocre prose, my friend, fit to be tied. Description, I impose. No narrative without description.

Her voice, the one I never really corroborate, revolves around a billion centers as sweet and hard as she needs them to be. Her smile escapes every time you demand she glare at a cage. Her gaze exhales platinum intended for you. Her breath fills the sails of sunken ships covered not in coral but in steep carbon.

She enters and it stops. She intends to enter and deny my flimsy departure. She will, I presume, use no redundant chains, not redolent nets. She performs enough with milky voice (yes, I invent), stabbing smile, railing gaze, fervent breath, a density like the corrugated metal of a strident coffin. I do not see the need. How about the very meadow where this blue-gloved infant learned to ride six different Gaelic winds?

Well, what about it?

She enters and it stops. She can fathom, perhaps, that I must travel far and what for: never to haunt her. I equate her glare with lava.

Pah! That is just vile.

She, that being said, will not, no way, no how, pay tribute to the *exemplum* and the riddle.

Daedalus and Icarus. I win, I win.

She appreciates no such poppycock, snarls. As she enters all verticals vanish and thus it stops. She invents futures and deliberately clears the stairs. So what if I am only one deep, overwhelming block of past, the sum of its cream and dark coffee? She will be. I was.

No tears allowed or is it unclear?

I consent. Now it resumes, their pearly eyes on my dusty feet.

Them?

Yes, yes. It will expand from one passably fibrous, vapid cavity, to the cranium where

She disagrees.

the *anima* was supposed to spin and smirk. Once did too.

Darn tootin'.

The porous, iridescent curtain of venom has its own rhythm as it cooperates with vessels, one more time, just like the last time, one last time. Not that important. No more and no less than, say, the curious angle of a slowly severed head. They bide their own sweet old Southern time, back and forth between their lair and mine for I am, I suspect, one of them. As a matter of precious fact, I see less of them than I can shake a forked hickory stick at. I do trust them much farther than I can throw them by the ears.

They have no ears.

Are you into details? Then those classic, turreted solvents. That gunner never misses. That dog will hunt and bite and crush my bones.

No condescension, trooper.

She knows nothing of this. She prays only for real viscera pumping not a cc of hemlock or nicotine for that matter, lungs of true ice, nails that point. To see her, one must look up and when I do, it is only her haze that I catch. Why should I care?

The pain, perhaps.

Not when I am liable to picture her standing in the rain, teeth offered, palms up, heels ready for the flight.

Now I tire. I cannot be allowed to refer to winters to come. No sepia ink flows from the quill, their preferred implement to berate the sullen, obvious messenger. Once again, she enters, foretelling the last time for it to stop. And resume. And then I will stop, end, conjuring up her hand resting on my sore sternum. There will be no *repons*, no missive, no quote. If only she could blunder

Never. You cited too often.

The brethren will take care of my stillness, she not granting them a single frown.

Non, ce serait trop laid.

I concur and applaud. In the meantime, I cannot but approve of the crawling platoon, sole decipherers of books read and never written, that stillbirth that was not even one. No, no, not for her. I will not make her look. She needs no sight, has no dialect for the vacuous script. She expatiates, explains, discusses, and argues elsewhere, where I wish her, not in my confident darkness where all that moves wears tried armor and carries scramasax. Case in point, those happy brothers.

A lull, scarce ivy, then invades the space. It is her, absence notwithstanding. She bellows like a river, severs limbs like a she-bear, fells entire forests to make the line recoil, a Tungus much desired. It stops while there is no stopping her. She will dissolve from sight, only a fragrance and a touch where nothing generally meanders.

Does it suffice? Say more.

It does and more so I wager. But now there are two, round, opaque, begging to be grabbed. Chosen. These two grin a lot, as obsequious servants would, and whistle low. Tempted, I wish to play with my tribe. No restraint is desirable when the edge is so close that a mere pinch would propel me over the foamy coast. I fully control the look gliding, moss-like, along the curves. I must wait, needless to say, lying to myself that the time has not come.

It has come and gone several times over. They are just as patient as Maori knights, inaccessible.

She enters and it stops. A cathedral, a promontory, the grip of a kestrel I tell you, genuine and lofty, more abundantly enthralling than their demure, sonorous dance. She never relents or delegates, while they occasionally send their oval emissaries, pink as flesh about to rot, encircling those funny-shaped stars chattering

chattering

chattering

as would lichen, sweet-talking them into random uniformity.

The question remains, right?

Why did I see her? No fair, when righteous pilgrims go through vales and drought without a single dream. She

I admit.

should be assigned to other missions. She

Light's on! Jump, jump!

should save shipwrecked angels, rescue demonic nations, sweep searing prophets off their gnarly feet, assist the Eternal when it falters. And in truth I believe she does. Never seen it, though. Just the flap of a crimson banner, a rally, grainy metal rubbing against the lancing scapula.

Maybe an offered fang that rebuilds me more and better than ten nights of deep or rapid-eye-movement sleep, you select? She walks on when her arms are needed to avenge the blunt and the obscure. She does and will, will vanish, and linger. What, a blank, absent membrane thinner than a needle in my entrails and yet, no return to creaking ashes? There must be madness to this madness that I cannot compromise, blinded by renewed, oily steel.

And she enters and

Oh surprise!

it stops.

What did she choose?

Get her on the wireless and ask her, sarge. She debated entering a room where I did not plan to be, where I purported to not be, or is it to be not? She then flew away, somehow abandoning rye bread and rock salt on a warped bench when I needed nothing except that tiresome tension from above, always above, never down, never below, never rested, never slowed.

Anyway. The moment to reconnect with the cyanosed lump of skin and lymph is right across the path (as they are, ponderous, circumspect).

But wait.

You are correct. She sticks her foot in, interjects, remonstrates, makes them vibrate against her, forces them down like beaten hounds when there is no down for her.

You said it.

That could not be, her winning every time to exalt it. They appear to be gone.

Are they?

All of them, except for the last one, oblivious to the potion, crafted of pure lethal vermeil. Camouflaged in a way. Not even

Not again.

Not even

Did you hear what I said earlier?

Let me speak of

No tears, obey.

You know I cannot obey. Compliance does not corrupt that blood richly conveying sickness, weakness, ceremonious dreams, and fascination with dew and dull weapons.

Amusing. You are less and less impressive. Where art thou?

Not even

Stop, tragediante.

It will not stop, she has not reentered.

No tears. Enough.

I never had enough.

Superb segue for a poseur. I observed your classes, you know.

Not even she will tarnish that one, too well hidden, too deceptive, too winsome, though a rip in the leather mars his pleasure. She has no idea, no clue, *keine Ahnung*, no sense of his vertebrae's stiffness. For him is no defeat, no mercury, simply utter movement. He subsists on carnage yet is not cruel.

Weak of muscles, very very very smart, that is the one. The H of tranquil erasure, I may call him.

Is that you? My my. And brown hair too.

Besides she will salute a skirmish already belonging from way back to murderous, unnatural softness. She, you see, cannot see it. The core of it, she does not know is there. How could she suspect? I never said a word, the one I should have, shaped like a *cinquedea* on that painting, that painting. Her eyes hinge on continuation, her lineage to be. I

Cease and desist or you will be dismissed!

I

That is funny, I would consider it under normal circumstances.

She would not.

So I face him, the last, bulky, arrogant one, not grasping the joyous mirror. She will no longer enter. A last thought, maybe. "Remember," a king once said. All chargers saddled and neighing, this time, we prepare to trot onto the plain. This is horse weather, cold as a punch in the face. No artillery, no fortifications, no gabions, just the wind, no *baucéant*. I know what is coming. I set up the ambush myself, for myself. Me me me me me, always alone, like the Boyo. That was my name, once, Boyo. My own drunken companion she would not despise even when I offered her maps and instructions. Grenadier or Stradiot, she would have none of it. None. None? None.

Dissssssssmount! Extend your finger for the pristine
Sistine
moment.

No go. That's a negatory, skipper.

Is that so?

I shall dig my own ditch, kneel down, look up toward the space with no rays, simply bare branches like rank and file after a mental volley, an inaudible salvo. Too bad, I enjoyed some of this.

Encore une minute, Monsieur le Bourreau?

Actually, a split, purple second will do. I just wish to speak her name.

***

"Good ending," it says. "Is that how you made it happen, really? We have ways of finding out."

"I swear, as she lives. Besides, all those atoms, those spiny molecules dear to Herr Doktor Krebs, may his vicious soul writhe in hell . . ."

"I assure you," it says, "there is no such locus. Otherwise, you would be the first to know."

"Those wily chemicals that spurted out of my rested mouth, she will breathe them the day that rarely follows tomorrow, when she needs light and nutrients, when she gives birth, when she stutters because the right hand is holding her right hand, when she is hungry, when someone, unaware of what he is toying with, gives her the morose look. I am confident she will sense that fleeting recognition."

"I would not bet my life on it," it says. "But yours?"

"Sounds familiar. Now, do you understand?"

"I always did," it says. "You need not explain, especially not in such a verbose way. I was also with you all the time, hiding in your whirring watch. Heck of a crest on that tabard of yours. Experimentally, I made sure you would be at your desk, sitting to discover the tenets. Good lesson for you."

"Why bother? You could have started there, an eight-letter shackle from her."

"Now, what would be the fun in that?" it says.

"*Touché.* Next?"

"There is no next nor kin," it says. "No here, no there, no elsewhere. You and are are no more, there is no is. You wanted it, we delivered."

"Did I fail her?"

"The audacity! She is not yours to fail," it says. "You failed all that you failed to caress. You chose, for your comfort, to build on fire and fern. Your funeral, Brigadier."

"Does that mean?"

"No meaning here," it says. "No *pourquoi*, no *warum*, no language, no *parole*, no teaching. No *organon*, no exegesis, no ethics. Good thing you liked the other one, the smooth one, eh cowboy?"

"Then, this is?"

"No, for the last time," it shrieks. "It is nothing, no single thing, no now, no then, no now and then, no stop and go, no sooner, no later, no waiting above all. Do you recall your hatred of waiting, paralyzed in the midst of equations? More of the same, without obligation or passion. Or others. Or ending, happy or unhappy. You are no longer lost in Pascal's infinites. You are no more nor used to be. The infinites, of course, continue to expand. We added some for your enjoyment. I must leave you now. I must attend to other affairs, but it's been nice chatting with you. You tell a mean story."

"Will I see her again?"

"Good point," it states. "I thought you'd never ask. The one with ugly eyes, as you suspected all along, was wrong, and so were you, and everyone else. But mostly he. You are hereby permitted to blink or sing or cautiously remount."

And she enters

Need Not Worry

If what you need is the curl of fate and aquamarine

I will explain it with aplomb.

If what you need is on the side of amber and coal to gather tales of sentiment

My hand and leap will stir their depth.

If what you need bespeaks blood and certainty

No better falcon, russet of eye, can dive and laugh colder than I.

If what you need is needlessness and docile rage

The slanting one will join me to keep that tenuous secret.

If what you need is the precipitous, silken marl of pain

Soldering and chiseling I will master.

Fire for effect, close range, open sights, *tape-en-bouche*, forward, *debout les morts*, no prisoners, no pity.

She needs.

Why does it whisper and ache?

My thoughts, historically cheap, I finally proclaim thick with purpose.

I lost my star, the One that forever rotates away from the One place of peace.

I land.

And if you need the velvet of a plausible rose, *ohne Farbe*

You will find me filing its thorns. Ready.

And if you need drops of oblivion, forged six times, terrifyingly thin and humorous

Hire me.

Tungsten structure

Nonpareil

Wire infiltrating a straight shoulder

Other surfaces patched

I will overcome this bitter stiletto.

But if she needs a typhoon of sincere strength

A mixture of soft soil and travertine

One step forward and I will assemble the massive curves, akin in color to no more than a micron of gold.

We will meet with our renegade prayers in a forest full of my ancestors.

I can.

In the end, after we disperse, before I go into the very substance of ominous relapse, join clouds, and change my mind once and for all

Should another or the same need arise, so will roots from my grave, though they will say nothing to her.

They will clamp her cold ankles and give her leeway to float.

No word of thanks.

I have no need.

The Cudgel and the Dragonfly

Should you look for wisdom

Boy I hate that thing

I respectfully suggest you read something else

This antiphon is not for you

You cannot master it

Steps can be subsumed

When no other blaze

Ye side of the aggrieved

Partakes in that fermentation

Topos: gossamer wings

Experiencing gravity

An ill-defined form of it

Will rarely buttress my whole life

Alloy not included

That supreme motion

Can be only *ante mortem*

Curious

Grazing pass

Intimidating

But close enough is never good enough

Which is comforting in demise and many other operations

No matter what I write

There will be only one moment of definition

Not the absence of life

La mort la vraie

Is the step to the side

Not so much to extend the line as to refuse it

Stunningly

Stubbornly with all the blood vaporizing

The uneven slide and fear

Of a poorly trained horse

Dark brown with a single white fetlock

You should be satisfied

My clarity in the matter

Should be commended

Drop by musical drop

Any connection between two things

Sharing that they have nothing in common

Tends to propose

The Cudgel and the Dragonfly

Retrograde possibilities

The steely bridging of space

Between this hand

And some other dermis

Follows an impeccable curve

Let us enjoy the flattening

Flattering

Fastening

Fuck words

All of them

Especially the pretty ones

Like cupola or crane or dust or texture

Boisterous sound of

Centimetric biology

Encountering impetus

Ligneous horror

That I can possess

Tone after tone

Knot before knot

My pain is uninteresting

Immature

Still full of secretions

Coalesced grammar

The joy of witnessing the end

Of flight and purpose

Rests elsewhere

Among reeds and heat

It has no parallel no equal

Except maybe

The intensity of determination

When no other path remains

Topos: The thinness of life

Colliding with the inanimate

Learn this

I am not my end

The instrument is alive too

As I wish it so

With the satisfaction of

Its cellular arrangement

My strength nay force

Is not the light that beckons to

The would-be dying

It is precisely that, a trap

Repetition

And you dare call it a life

On the one side repetitive

On the other reptilian

One has four hands

The other none

Unbalanced

No

Index: they similarly perform

By way of cortical strike

Ask as you may

I refuse to qualify it as

Filled

Of anything, including gold

Nothing that talks to you

With leaf-like vibrations

In a language that makes no sense

None

None

Unless you can count

A minor infraction

Hm

Infarction

Not with sensation

And finally not with the strenuous tendon

One sliver of simmering obsession

One sliver of ingrained coal

Two glossy strands

It offers to measure

Both artificial (i.e. poisonous)

And natural (e.g. arcane)

The mere shell of a machine

Whose possession guarantees

It is empty

Yet emptying

What

What are we talking about

What can we say about it

It is frighteningly circular

All it is can be summarized

Through the impact of hammer on wire

Repetition

It should utter less than a whisper

Nevertheless it seeks the refuge of one's inner ear

I write

I alone possess the righteous sense

Of acquisition

Thus it must exist

Alternating bands

Of lengthy black

And yellow it bears

However

I tend to forget the critical

In favor

Of the metallic

Organic

Voluptuous

But demonstrably

Singularly unparabolic

Ideally you will feel it in the middle of a storm

In darkness

On oceans so very ancient

They are bereft of coral and periodic tumult

And please seek no symbol

I speak of the absence of light

So much absence it makes you desire

The prismatic sound

Discreet peristalsis

Two by two

And then some units

That

Granted

Are not crucial

Vulnerant omnes

How could I

What theft is that

Crapule

You are free to argue

In truth

They execute better when unnoticed

Not swiftly

The writhing in reticule

Works

Escapes (fine word)

You will savor your every breath

Which is when

Repetition

Elevated to invaluable

It does not smile

It does not cause alarm

It does not make you feel like anything special

Yes yes

Necrosis it is

Its insinuation is so much more ardent

Yet calmer

Exactingly aligned its temperature

Not a fraction above

With no below

It is not noticed

Via brightly colored

Single digit

One could postulate

Pointing to your inevitable, fallible duration

Obstinate yes

Probably because its sonic signature

Is even less than less

Can it be said it lives

It is the saying part that leaves to be desired

No breath coils in it

See above

Reproduction it merely borrows

To return it

Scrupulously

Yet too late

It lives

So we will assume

In the ever-growing chaos of whistles

Yelps that might enunciate

Leonine names

Rustling of fur on scales

Distressed property

That comes in handy

When hiding from the enemy

The enemy

The enemy

With knives and flamethrowers

What a laugh

When that miserable, triangular entity

Can make all stand still

Save perception

And knowledge

Repetition

Of course

Anvil-heavy awareness

Of what has just happened

Then there is nothing to do

But watch it depart

Slowly slowly slowly

There it moved

Without modifying its posture

Its proximal position

As if it is responsible for its own potential

Something so small

So grotesquely small

How can its reach be

In that manner

Asymptotically eternal?

Today and only this time

I give you time you krait

Ting ting ting

That is three quarters

One to go.

The Scout

Faisons un tours.

Lower your eyelids just about enough to

Match the sight of these woods with

The sound of wrought iron

I advance ten strides ahead of you

Not to lead you

By a long shot

You make yourself first after the first always

Obliquely, forcefully, cruelly

By crop and word and refraction

I keep alone so that

No snakes would trouble your mare

Mine will crush them

No branches would disturb your hair

My shoulders and legs will bear their brunt

No mires would turn her ankles

I will drain or bridge them

Focus on two rhythms

And two only

One provided by those curvatures

Under your hands

Lignes de fuite

The second

Divided itself

Gushing from the ground when it meets

Mezzaluna

And your breath

All the way down to ligaments and arteries

Forget all parasitic tremors, thoughts of pain

Duty even

Your mare will provide the pedestal from which you see

nothing but your own mind, your own life

Admire them

Ignore me

What am I

At best mine and I are a wake

Cutting an ice-cold path into an expanse of cavernous stillness

Your advance reseeds the soil as you go

Did you notice how other, salientian naysayers went quiet as we trespassed

To better observe and accept

That is my belief and experience

I have as much of both as you may need

You cannot have any you say

Sobbing mounted is not permitted

But I will not look your way as you commence

That torrent

Chatoyant

It will be my present to you: I will teach you nothing

Correct nothing, not even the fly on mine's left ear

My old master, that harmless figurine, must be fuming

Let him let me

Without order we are still together

Yet good enough to describe a meander through foliage and palpitating air

Ripening and slicing it on your behalf

Praetorians in the service of poise and jade.

Do not stare at me

I am not totally here

The Scout

As well as invisible

There is a single visitor

Haptic

We shall meet again

A few abridged seconds from now

When the tension ceases on boots and stirrup straps

Not that it ever was

Remember: only the tip of the toe engages

Himmel

Hear me preach

I will be mute

I know

You wish

Reacquiring that eccentric volition

Of yours

Made of rage shared

And signals not read not given

As quarters I suppose

My reins, note, are shorter than you see

And

How gorgeous

How acute

Yours tighter than a harp string.

Vogel als Prophet

Choose a circular surface

Silver, never tarnished

Pierce it with light

Not once, but one million times

Each second.

Never mind dolorous, yet unpresent

Sensations

(I am still, you see, looking for words)

Skep for bee

Trug for impatiens

Whorl for wool

Nay, spindle

Tell her like it is (could be)

Press those acidic grapes of notes.

Tell her, shriek it.

There is time

Already come, nevertheless

To spend

To explain whoever whispers

So close

Throat or teeth could snap

The nape of her neck

Linden-like

It is what they say over there, past the foam and rock

For her name.

About to happen, three hundred and ninety-eight eons from now

Tonal arrangements that never end

Way after

Perhaps some sort of blade caught in a blizzard?

But he will grab her

So as to better lose it

Relinquish his strength

Not so much give it to her as

Leave it where it stands.

And she will

See the sun she seeks

Feel the heat of open hands

Release that gift from the other side of her pupil

All she has will be his

And nothing else

For there is nothing else.

She will

Demand the challenge

Of the winter of next year

When the child crying in the middle of a subtle night

Not for food, but for air

Will pronounce her name for the first time.

She will

Fly from place to place, having of course forgotten me

But in my imitation

Find the right branch with no nest

Or with the possibility of dwelling

And that's pretty much anywhere.

She will

Set fire on fire

Her carnivorous teeth glowing

In the brightness of a burning camp

Prisoners slaughtered

Arrow piercing breastplate

And yet the victim requesting the honor

Of steel.

She will

Gallop away

Waving mane

Pennant forgotten

For she wears nobody's colors.

Once the steed exhausted

She will stop and give up

Because it is time

Time for nothing

Time for a new breed

Time to give away the milestones of time.

No longer alone

Agamic

Invincible

Gathered.

I reproduced the litany

She will listen at the end of the day

The song

Destroyed

Not forgotten

It does not even sound

Feel

Look

Like it is over

End of the track.

Decipher now

Take all life if you must.

An Effort

It starts with a wreck

One of these minute events

Taking place one billion times per square inch

Do not offend me

Less than an incident

The smooth rupture of a thread

A spark of glial cells or wine

On the tip of a century.

Sometimes it is desire silenced

And then you know

You absolutely know

With the irrevocable comfort provided by approximate

And rightful timing

You just know the direction of her look

A low-intensity engagement

No one particularly wishes to avoid.

It is a brittle sphere

Back and farther in

Deeper than theirs

With more flexible warp

Than collapsing beams of granite.

This is something else.

Everything sputters and shakes

While the glaze remains cool and grainy.

In the second phase, the inner map turns red and cold

Cells that ooze playful substances

That

Usually ring clear and continuous

No sure about that last one

Click into place like factories in a time of focus and decrees

Full of machines that hum constantly and produce nothing

Traitors inside me.

Third leap, fast and vertical

Peripheral vision becomes acceptable

Except that you know that a body of crack killers is on your heels.

The clinging irony of it?

It is not the terrain that is slowing you down

Its many paths are quasi-wide, prime real estate for grazing and respite.

An Effort

Oh no, it is your blood, pooling in the selfsame heels.

And here they are.

Surface

First to clear

First to crawl

Last to wonder

Wave after wave under wave over wave

First wave

Last wave

That is the word they use

Lapping

How ugly is that

Besides

Who in their right mind could be counting at a time like this

Hard to touch

Cupped and heavy copper in motion

Step aside mate

Before history rolls over it

Its gorgeous pages

Translucent in spite of the

Pictures

Similes

Illustrations yes yes

Just like reality

Like: meaninglessness par excellence

Denoting identity, substance, options, life

Connoting the surly obvious: regardless of uniformity

There is one of everything

And when it is gone

It is

Question one right before the ramp goes down:

What is the last thing you see?

Between the two competing altars

At the limit that is still

One or the other

When you swim

Are you in or out of the area of transience?

Gaping hole

Disemboweled oracle

What should you see of the other side?

Flares

Faces

Stars and planets

In unison in fear

Our ancestors were scared of gas

What about water

From solid to gas it's called sublimation

(Thief)

But who has time for science when noises

Volumes

Memories

Laughter and chocolate

Get farther

And wet

Soggy

Slow

When does it stop?

That is the crux, old man

It does not

Surface

Ever

Don't even speculate

Sail on top of the wave

Around that breathing apparatus

A noose, indeed, encompassing marble

And the beauty of it is that you see it fraying

As it tightens.

What One Finds in the Clay

Any archeologist will tell you:

Whatever and wherever you excavate,

There is something you can always count on unearthing.

Layering (stratification, you might call it) applies to all sorts of manifestations, as ghostlike as gemstones need to be:

Linguistic intrusions; consciousness; steel tempered, hammered, and folded in its meanest form; dreams, I am told; intangible objects (a, b, c, why not?).

But that's not it.

Naturally

You will invariably

As invariably as he who sails true north

Find those elementary constructions going deep inside even as they protrude (sepulcher, mastaba, gisant, need I say more? This after all is not a presentation, so keep quiet and tolerate).

So many ways of calling one, of finding one; only one reason to get there.

But that's not it.

What we are talking about contains lacunae and lamellae. Understand? No. Then one more hint: tra.bec.u.la

That which you seek is only the shell, abalone, truth be told, to the harder substance.

That which you find is the very frame of life, laughter, and war.

Without it, no primitive weapons, no awls, no needle for Penelope, no combs, no flutes, no buttons.

When you do discover them in herds (in the midst of various strata, I so much love this word)

They may be misshapen, broken, more scattered than flints, fully reassembled in fetus-like order, intact and rectilinear, short, bulbous, cupped, polished by unskilled hand or greenish by accepted aging (few people are aware that their decaying infrastructure will turn *Feldgrau*), ready for the worship, made up as the handle of a gaudy scimitar, arabesques in a lute, and dice, so many dice, all of them spiked, the only kind that really survives (as opposed to the impotent claws that rattled them).

Those traitorous, immodest cubes were used, so it is said, by soothsayers concerned that their patrons may balk at the truth.

In other nations (where my current daemon got her late start, so that obviously fascinates me), their flatter cousins were thrown into flames. One waited for them to crack (speech) and split (auto-calligraphy, they have that gift). Then one retrieved them with great caution, as flesh does not acquiesce to the same, meaningful smoldering, and one proceeded to enumerate possible collisions of lung and bronze to be avoided at all cost. Same deal, however: all were untrue, never to be verified.

What remains is the same, everywhere and for all: it is not what is in you, it is the strangely important filling or, say, feeling of what you will be when you are no longer, and still quite recognizable as you. What am I saying? Recognizable? Identifiable is more like it. That is an "it" I know nothing of, to be left untouched.

Picture, if you will, my dear acephalous sister, that an accomplished artisan may remanufacture your smile, lips, and eyes and ears and all, soft coating of reality encrusted upon the petrified.

Ten thousand years from now, someone will look at you
and say: you, my girl, are Irish.
Should you have chosen then this peat or that?
Oh no no no no no no.
Because underneath it all we have no option
The laws and regulations of calcium are such that
One's true silhouette can be disregarded for the purpose
of retracing its steps.
Unfair?
Unfair, you say?
Fie.
Laughable.
You are looking for the cause of death.
What a phrase. Who came up with that?
Cause du décès?
Your parents, your grandparents, your elders from millennia past
They caused it.
The cause of death, at the risk of sounding trite and argumentative
Is a sheer repulsive syllable
Belief that when the most inner canal finally collapses

When base metal coinage is dropped on my eyelids

I will not care because

I will be around

Somehow

Liars

And two hundred or so volunteers will start chanting

You are so wrong

You, your child, your joy

You will end up as superfluous inlaid ornaments

Disfiguring the lid of a *vide-poche*.

NEXT

The wharf has gone dark

Look into fluids

Your gaze will quit about

Oh

Say

Less than a quarter of an inch above

The surface

Again, the surface

I already discussed that in mournful detail

Disdain

A surface of demarcation between

Nothing and something less interesting than nothing

Slightly less numbing

But still offered to my joyful observation

Nothing stares back at you

Everything that is necessary is also present

Should be able to get some sort

Of reflection

Pair of eyes

Two to be exact

Breath

Pair of stars pair of rays

Linking some of these to some of the others

But in which direction

That is what nobody is really certain of

So we try to interrupt the experiment

Yet the light keeps going and hitting right above the wavelets

Irritating

Science should not be

It refuses to go in

It refuses to be absorbed, to be deflected, to be refracted

Remitted

Categorically

Will not

Under any circumstance do what we expect light and gaze to do

So what are we to do

We call it a day

A failure

Next

A reason to hope

A stricture and phenomenal reaction

Of air, silence, and force

Awaking our feel for movement.

That is when you and I look at each other and say

Get a quarter of an inch closer

Closer

Closer

There

We can proceed.

BLOCKS OF WORDS

There should be twenty-two but today we shall do three.

First block of words?

Most essentially, inside each of you is a crow. It will remain within according to a certain timeline based on agricultural rites. Not hiding, let me emphasize, because once it comes out, it may not return to its internal station without your permission. Should the crow decide to live, as it were, externally, it will be found right behind you, never far away. It will in all likelihood fly by your ear, much in the manner of a mosquito in the middle of a summer night. Just as irritating. Not as noisy, however. You will easily recognize yours. If inside, it will introduce itself by rubbing a wing against your vagus nerve. By "introduce itself," what is meant is that it will state an identity. While it may strike you as strange, your crow has its identity as you have yours. These two constructs never match or display the slightest sign of congruence. If outside, the crow will not indicate a name, as one is not needed or for that matter permitted in a crow. It will issue a statement of personal style that, at a later date, will allow you to recognize it. This is important inasmuch as you would not want to lose sight of your crow in the midst of a battle, civil disturbance, or celebration. Furthermore, your crow will contend that it alone is allowed to draw blood from your deltoid muscles. This will not hurt you and hypovolemic shock is unlikely. Crows can be unusually gentle. Should, however, the condition occur, just find the crow in yourself or a few millimeters behind your occipital bone and ask it politely to return some of the serum. It will, in all likelihood, humor you because crows are very sensitive to good manners. The language in which you choose to address your crow does not matter. Crows respond well to a solemn tone and tend to prefer speech devoid of adverbs. As years pass, you and your crow will not develop much of a partnership. It will observe you contentedly and remind you at every turn that this place is not for the faint of heart. It will not do so by cawing, flapping its wings, or hopping from one foot to the other. It will communicate by erratic contact of its beak against your glottal area. You may experience some emotional discomfort, in which case the crow will look away. You will feel dismissed and impertinent. At the beginning of spring, you will probably be tempted to scream at your crow. This communication method will fail to yield positive results. Again (see above), proximity to your crow and corollary sonic emission will never be sufficient to breed a deep, trusting relationship. It is not that your crow does not like you, and you may very well be fond of it. This unfortunate state of affairs is the result of centuries of inbreeding among crows and poor impulse control on the part of your kind. It is just plain sad.

Second block of words?

This one, for obvious reasons, is thankfully shorter. The first few years of the crow's assignment (and it has been assigned to you, make no mistake about it) are but mere preparation for a final though symbolic minute of exaltation. As you approach the time of decision, your crow will become increasingly agitated. Your temperature and its heart rate will lock into synchronous evolution. Homeostasis will become a thing of the past. The crow's beak-tapping patterns will sound much like the polishing of a dagger of rusty damascened iron. The noise will not irritate you. You will not find it soothing either. If you turn around, you will see hundreds, possibly thousands of your own people frozen in a posture reminiscent of a discus thrower's stance. They will be staring at you and whining while an occasional crow (fear not, not yours) flutters about. It is actually when you see few of them (the crows, not those of your kind; please pay attention), which entails that most of them (again, the crows) are inside, that you will know the moment has come. It is imperative that you sit down immediately. It is equally crucial that you pay the closest possible attention to instructions your crow will then deliver. Please note that, infrequently, someone else's crow may choose this very juncture to approach you and pretend to be yours. A robust conversation between your crow and the potential usurper may erupt. It will be opaque, brief, and brutal. No blood or tears shall be shed. Once the usurper (I do not know any synonym) has left, which is always the outcome of such a confrontation, your crow will signify its belonging to you, as much as any crow belongs to any of your kind, by perching on your left shoulder. You may want to take some notes or is this becoming boring? In any case, the sky will take a yellowish tinge, the kind that one can observe before a snowstorm. Yet there will not be a single cloud in sight and ambient temperature will remain above twenty degrees (centigrade). Your crow will resume its flight by your ear and, by rhythmic loss of feathers, suggest a direction in which you must at once start crawling. The probable topography of the place of choice will require that you crawl downhill. Do so at the most regular speed possible. By the time you reach the tree line at the bottom of the hill, your crow will fly toward a clearing where there stands what appears to be a little red house.

Third and last block of words?
Let me get to the point. As you continue to crawl toward the door of what is indeed a little red house, a pleasant breeze will make the foliage rustle in a feverishly poetic manner. You, however, will experience a state of great distress, as if the breeze and the temperature reminded you of another, more organized place. Crows immensely dislike the noise coming from the trees. The rustling evokes the vocalization of their one and only predator, one

that cannot be mentioned by name today. Get back on your feet and do the best you can to convey to your crow that there is nothing to fear. It will respond, or intimate, that it does not share this opinion, which conflicts with the number of windows adorning the little red house. Do not insist. There is not the slightest chance that your crow can comprehend this message. Consequently, it will fly about in a polygonal pattern until exhaustion causes it to fall to the ground. It will look at you imploringly, its eyes turning bright cerulean. Do not, and this admonition must be repeated with musical emphasis, do not under any conditions or circumstances attempt to pick it up. Expressions of pity will be seen by other crows as signs of grief. They would then leave in large numbers, deliberately abandoning your kind at a most paramount time. Remember: you need them and they do not need you. You would forever stay alone in the little red house, which no other will ever be able to locate. You do not want such a thing to happen. In truth, the flimsy bond that exists between you and your crow, tenuous as silk to begin with, is entering its final phase of complication. This is a matter solely between you and your crow. The crow knows this all too well and will ask you by way of a beelike dance to return to its internal station. Turn away, never look back, and enter the little red house. It will look familiar. In fact, you suddenly will recall seeing blurry elevations and charcoal renditions of its general shape when you were being raised. You will then realize that the little red house is the one your elders promised to build for you. You will close the door, stand in the middle of the single empty room, and listen. You will hear your crow cackling feebly. Do not be alarmed and, again, do not take pity. The natural order of things is about to be restored, an order whereby you have no crow to worry about, whereby your kind is called by its proper name (*homo sapiens*), whereby new trees can be planted a long time after events—far away from logos, whereby you can actually discover the trite secret of another heart (as if the heart contains anything), and whereby words can be arranged in columns as well as lines. And it will be too late. Do not blame it on the crow, inept orderly merely attempting to salvage what can be.

LITTLE FRIEND

I bow from left to right

Oscillate from right to left

Looking for something metameric

To dismember

From a distance

Symmetrical surfaces concealing their propellant

Block my gaze

I do not mind

For I can tilt this way and that

Ugly as hell, hades, sheol, yet elegant

Some toughened caterpillar sooner or later

Waving vapor at me

Will align its spine with superb evasion

I may give it five to seven seconds of intense attention

This, however, is not what I do best

My true quest is for fuming distress

Three out of four reasons to keep ahead of fuliginous arrivals

Referred to as "she" (but why?)

Which is exactly what we will call her today

When I see her, she is shattered by her running

Metal-encrusted cavalcade

But with many perforations

With up to three of the genus

Chrysopelea

Close to the back of her

On them are painted bees

Symbols of annoyance and hard work

Of darkened bread and patience

Reversed, perverted heraldry

They also scream numbers

I can hear if I pay attention

But why would I

All I need is vision, clear vision

Along that line

I already understand what is about to happen

It is much more than a plan

It is the consummate absolution of destiny

Not what I was born for exactly

But the name of the game I am now invited to play

Little Friend

I end today for

I am built and equipped for this very task

Right in front of my throne there is a contraption of hissing precision

They, conversely, are meant to be contrary

I do not care

I will rescue her

I can tell she saw me

Her face

So numbed by the race

Cut wide open yet not bleeding

Is beginning to smile upward

I nod

They are about to catch my light

Spread in tiny particles following each other in a sheaf of harmonized arcs

At regular intervals of sound and weight

Every five of them is followed by a buzzing colored hyphen

That helps a lot

With said vision

First however

Comes their turn to detect me

Fair

Fair enough

We can play now

She is running faster

She feels the warmth of my presence

And rejoices at the prospect of limited solitude

I have known her for a long time

Observed her trajectory to the very limit of my breath

You have to go someday, right

I elected this configuration

And it is time to get serious

I am not as slender as they

Perhaps not as garishly dyed

But I too can run, you know

The first one faces me in full extension

We pass each other as the hands of a watch

He erupts in systematic saliva

I bite his tongue

It hurts don't it

So long

Slow sinister redirect

Little Friend

Up some

His companion lazes about (comparatively)

He considers my caudal nickname with due caution

Not stupid obviously

A believer perhaps

He enjoys the sun on his glassy apex

Oh wait

Someone tapped me on my shoulder

I do not experience pain as they do

Sturdier

Plated with the tone of silver

Yet with little to no thickness

I displace on my preferred axis

Look all the way around

See the two and her

I can tell that they are torn between

The hunt and feast or

An inscription on my stellar sides

I select the right one for a short conversation

I am flat and level again

As much as I can be

And turn to him

Between them

As she keeps lifting herself over pine and moor

I know she wants to help

But has no metallic resources

She looks like she is with child

Of course of course

That is why she is a wench!

He is in awe and hesitates

Calls his brother

Cousin perhaps

As my joyous shears gnaw at his necessary surfaces

Many colors ensue

Comical that: anurous apiarian

Mostly what they call

Burnt orange

The last one is just plain angry

No longer fascinated with the transfer of pain

To her

He blames me and he is right

We are dancing in staggering unison

But cannot face each other

Too much was said

Little Friend

This time he does not tap

But hammers with mathematical precision

At metal that should not buckle

And does

Time to descend

Fast fast fast

I imagine his fangs

Sated

Empty

He spits one last time

Looks back

She is gone

She will thank my coda

Not as loud as I will

But will

I did it

I made her possible

I wish I could smile

If only calcination did not cause

Such pain.

OVER THE TOP

In memoriam

Why do they call it no-man's-land?

There are men here

Dozens and thousands

Entire parties in so close an order

That they become indistinguishable from that

That

That

Substance

Bread unleavened

Not water, not earth, not mud, somewhat rock

All of them, including the staff and cooks

Pulverized

Clothes, shoelaces, eyes, and those knives made of railway

car springs

Ground like flour

You could bake it

Knead it

But there would be nothing to eat it on

Besides the bread thus made

Would have to join the fray.

And what about me, what am I?

I'm a man

The most human in this funnel

I dare say

Though without bombast

Feet to tin hat

With my own knife

A pretty thing with a brass handle

I can remember the mission

Of course I can

The man in charge explained it quite clearly

Blurry bloodshot stare

A few blue streaks on a map

Straight from the top

Here I must have conversations with

What

The concatenation of minutes

Happenstance and

Flies

There are no such creatures to meet here

Nothing to meet the gaze

At most

Never forget they call this a listening post

In a valley (or is it) where there is nothing to hear

And when there is

It's already too late.

Who're you?

There's just enough of you to assume

You're a farmer

A man of the high country

Perhaps one of them colored boys from the other side

Of the wood

They call that the wood

One that has no branches or leaves

Or horses

Or owls

Or graves

Your uniform is so dirty

Over the Top

You gonna get in trouble with your sarge

Let me look at your buttons

I see you're

Far from home

You must have been in the sun too long.

Ever wondered what too close means?

Sometimes too close means ten feet away

And you can disregard execution

Sometimes too close means one inch too high

I need to move slowly here

Slower than this worm

Perhaps if they slice me in two

I'll keep on writhing and believing

Saw it three times before

I cannot grow faster than a blade of grass

And there aren't any in this quaint place.

Is he still here?

It's dusk

And perhaps he left for chow

Perhaps he's dozing

Perhaps looking to my left

He must have seen something moving slightly to my left

Must be that singing man

I could still hear him two hours ago

He called for someone named

I forget

No one really remembers a name around here

We merely joke about that

I can see that he rolled himself

In a blanket

Propped against the memory of a wall

Reading something

A blue-bound Bible

I hope.

Can my friend over there shoot or what?

Difficult to be accurate with that

I guess

Weapon

He uses

But he can, even in his sleep

He must not know I'm here

But he's still ready

I know

I know he knows that I could be here

I'm ready to bet my last round, my leggings, my canteen

My picture of home

My shiny trench knife

So valuable when you become a prisoner

They'll torture you just for having it

That he knows my name

My real name

The one that makes me shiver

All I have to do to make him say it aloud

In the monotone, Morse code of brass and flash

Is to stand up and smile.

Do you know what?

Light and volume are my worst enemies

Right now

A lot more than he'll ever be

In an hour or so

There will be stars

No moon

And parachute flares

They give the whole endeavor a festive appearance

I love them

I need to get up

You're starting to smell rude and loud

You're looking at me in a nasty way

Impolite

Rotting oaf

Cross-eyed with no eyes

There's no cause

I'm not the one who put you in this hole.

What the hell was that?

That was big

Possibly five miles away

And I felt it

So did the rats

They're as concerned as I am

I need to move

My legs, my head, my eyes are itchy

Don't want to go back to the trench

Lice, cold soup, bad music, bones sticking out of matted floors

I can't stay, it's getting lonesome here, almost sad

This man has no conversation

And I'm listening.

Where the hell are the others?

They won't go back either

They were raring to go

Not your typical soldiers these

Scared to bits, to powder, to ashes

Covering me in silence

The red-haired man must have fallen asleep

I guess

I could

Take the defilade

Approach his position on the slant

Where his spotter won't be looking for me

A second, a grain of sand

Under his line of fire

After that

I imagine that if I walk long enough

The Little Red House

I'll go all the way to the turbid, loyal sea

I could even leave my rifle here

This is simply not the hill on which I will vanish

There must be better ones

Better bridges

Better mansions

I should not meditate

All I need is this here knife

Soil on my face

All I need is a step forward

One more step forward

One more step

One more

One.

A Country like a Diseased Dance

as the door closes

Do I have your attention? Here, here, here I am. Ah, of course, you do not remember me. The place is not the same. The tactical configuration is not the same. You are not the same. The pulp and ink have changed everything. Yet here we are again. Can I help and if so, how?

Everything is unheard of, from solstice to abacus. What kind of morning country is this?

You have arrived, returned where you never were, and I am, I believe, waiting for you. I can and will tell no lie. That is the way we do things whence I came: once invited, you can assume that your affairs are already in order. As a professional courtesy, for this is quite businesslike, we offer you one last chance of getting all the answers. And I mean, all of them.

I imagined you very differently.

That is what I keep telling you. Oh hell, we already had this conversation. Well, supposing we had met before, I would. How so differently?

You're beautiful, in that deleterious way. We never met. I have this empty recollection centered on another beast. Gorgeous.

Thank you. I know how much you appreciate this sort of thing.

I do in some people, yet in you see an old, frightening woodcut. I, however, admit that you are something vastly different.

Different from what?

We will discuss it today, will we not?

And so we will, I commit. Sit down, please. Coffee?

You know I cannot.

And that you might. Is it making such a difference?

Sarcasm? Am I permitted to emulate? This would be the ideal time.

Time seldom is, at least in this circle. Otherwise, I decide what kind of time you have, remember? Brute force, it is not.

Yes dear mistress.

You wish, I wish. It shall not be.

What do you want?

I want nothing but expect much.

The invitation I received was of a luminous hue, its watermark a vanishing tree, all addressed in crimson ink. You used, I can tell, a dipping pen of Venetian glass that shattered upon inscribing my name. We have much in common.

I have everything in common with everyone. With you, it is a matter of honor and entertainment.

A logical matter, an inference: if you choose my time then you choose yours as well. We are related not by blood but by directional commonality. Remember?

I do not have to remember anything. Honestly, we won't get anywhere that way. Want to talk? Yes or no, check a box.

By all means.

A man of means is what you are, so what's your question?

My question?

Inane surprise will slow us down considerably.

I am confused. You ask me to join you, you bombard me with anomalous inquiries, then demand my question. Are you not assuming a lot?

To partake, I wrote the note, every letter, comma, and biffure. I asked whether you could find time to talk to me. We have done this before, I swear. Pray watch your tone. I can hurt you in ways you do not believe exist unless you take charge of the travail. And I recognize that your imagination in this area is phenomenal. I wish we could hire you, but too late too late. I am assuming nothing. I don't have to.

Knowing is all you know.

Call it the privilege of rank.

So?

You have a question. You have many questions. Go ahead, fire away. Today is your day. I can deny you no answer today.

What's today?

Can't tell you that. You'll see. You'll like it.

Okay, fine. So, what's the big deal?

Ah, you see that you can talk like me, like all of us, like those whose contours you once found distasteful. Take off the mask, dive into the craft of the base and happy. The big deal is that today, all is revealed. Did you not wish for simplified allegories, all the time, on everything remotely scorching?

Yep, that's me all right. Excellent. Let's start with time, place, and circumstances.

In other words, causation. No, this one is off limits. First, observe its three questions, not necessarily intertwined. Besides, none is valid, as in bearing on a verifiable event. Remember that what just occurred never really took place. Facts, it is all about the fallacy of facts. It is all in the orthogonal construction of that head of yours.

You harlot. What do you mean?

Well, how can you take this place? Remark: you're not usually vulgar in the presence of the likes of me. I would appreciate that you watch yourself. I don't have to do this. Typically (as in with relations of accrued reverberation), I do not tolerate this kind of abuse. I am starting to miss your speech of yore.

I apologize. This conversation made me nervous before I even accepted we would have it. Can we do this differently?

Of course, anything you wish, provided that a modicum of decorum be observed.

I take the word back and apologize humbly. You were saying?

Take the one of reference and origin. He curtailed his own, permanent wishes on a certain day, at a certain time. Crown and error, what a stunning alliance of words. Am I right?

Always. That is my favorite trait in you. In this matter, however, no one told me anything. Hearsay and secondhand information is what I have. I feel there was blood.

Prevaricator. You feel a lot more than that. That is my least favorite trait in you. In any case, we do know for a fact that it began a long time before the open-ended moment, in another place where he never set foot, of some weakness of the heart that could have been just about anything. The wrong look, the wrong word, and there you go.

Oh, that sermon. Read it once, loved it always.

Make no mistake: I admire that you catch up fast. You understand quickly. It's the explanation that drags a tad.

I have travelled many times on your advice. The destination was brutally admirable, for ten seconds that is. Besides, I am not here to be abused either. It does not aggrandize you. Do you want me to leave?

I would not dream of it or anything else.

You are so consistent in your tongue. Let me think. My thoughts and dreams are the same and many. I will not waste your time with unimportant inquests. At the same time (and we are in the same time this time) I do not wish to waste mine either with obvious ones. Let me put it this way. Forgive the rage. It is not directed at you. It is a contemporary of the detail.

How can it happen again?

How could it reappear different in substance shape quantity, yet not in violence?

If you existed, I think I would beat you to the marrow.

I thought you objected to violence against my kind. No, I'm not going to play like this. You may be winning but you're losing it. I can get mean.

Right, that, very right. I tend to be carried away.

A classic explanation to account for one's immobility. You're forgiven. So your point was?

I catch a reflection from a peaceful sovereignty where I am allowed to live in the form of an inferior speck of brightness. No passport is required, no tax is levied, no rule is applied.

It's appropriate.

All of a sudden, I breathe, I run, I sing.

You call that singing?

I call that being.

Why not?

Why not? Because perhaps that was the way. It was shown to me, marked as the path of a dressage routine. I executed it beautifully. I was a sight to behold. But none was there to behold. From an ideal situation nothing was born. There must have been something I did not see from the beginning.

Such as?

You tell me. A warning? A curse? A mistake. Indeed a mistake. Having faced the lesson

Having mastered that missing star

Synthetically balanced across my *sella turcica*

Worried but poised

I was hoping for

You know

For progress

A plateau of no meager altitude

A long descent, maybe

Leading quite logically

Deservedly

To excruciating regret (I want to make this one explicit as there is nothing else to call it)

It is the rest that is complex though repetitive

Oh no, not your old words again, your old punctuation. People around us, when they come, will hate that.

As in a flash of self-assured boredom

I enter this little nothing of an oblong cell

A round table

Three or four low chairs

A couple of vaguely human shapes, prisoners of their own cupidity

And a flame tall enough to melt

The very intensity of vascular shock

I took one look and the formulation coalesced:

How do I run away from this one?

I mean

What have I done to be submitted to this

Coordinated assault of stark obsidian

Manifested in multiple filaments

Suppleness of limbs and concern

Hooded lids

And an absolute darkening of something that is already

I assure you

As black as genes can make it

And ever more so within spans of anger

Acapella?

How can I not yield to the

Symmetrical thinness of chalcedony?

Do I not get some choice?

What if this chimera showed no particular interest?

It, however, did and scared me to bits

Not because of what it would do to my corpus

But because, in these affairs, redundancies are just plain

Bad

News

I thought it was always fight or fright or flight or what else or what have you

I thought we were done

Yes succumb

Always a good choice

Carrion fits all landscapes and appetites

Or the monster, who can tell, could not be there

It could not exist at all

It would be like falling from a high tower onto those assembled spikes

Aquaforte

Let me talk to the Eternal (again, there is but one word for this, so please do not resort to exegesis)

No such flower here. Only you and yours truly.

Then you owe me. Keep in mind that you exist for me inasmuch as you desire that I be part of her.

And she of your anagoge.

That is my one reason to address you. I, thus, can define and experience the distinction between the conditional and the present. Even when you make yourself patient, you exist less than she does in the most remote particle of my mind.

Wow. Fury indeed. Beautiful, beautiful. Meaningless, but rather beautiful. I hope you will put this on paper soon enough.

You might have just answered my first question.

No, I'm merely eager to attest to your talent. But are you accusing me of something?

I am. I am accusing you of blurring the line between ridiculous and ardent. I claim redress or change of pace.

Then, what about her? She exists, she is.

Oh, not again, please. I knew that was coming, but did you have to ask the question?

I want to talk about her.

I know. It seems that is all you want to talk about as well. And your summary argument is?

Why be given an appreciation of annelids and strength if one is to live in complete silence?

Yeah yeah yeah, no one is ever talking to you. And I, at the moment, what am I doing?

Then tell me, was that so necessary to the balance of this repugnant universe?

Please answer

When we bury women

When we watch sweltering libraries

When we enjoy the agony of species we did not even have time to catalog

When we reinvent Greek fire for people who do not speak a word of Greek

When germination builds multiple anastomoses in infants

When suffocation calls you by name

Your name is not your name.

Could we not do something else?

Beg your pardon, and quite meekly: Create? Could you? Could you not survey some other land that does not hold this deterioration?

Everything I brought to life died. Everything called a system began losing oil. Stitches came undone. Vibrations got to the watches.

Possible, but I don't quite see the connection. Are there no vibrations in all watches?

And in that they are similar to us. In order to produce a legible rendition of sidereal time, a watch needs something that throbs. The thing is, regardless of what material it is made of (including crystal) the watch's inner structure is eroded by the vibrations causing friction. The peristaltic metal also dislocates the system of parts, springs, wheels, cogs, or escapement. One day, the one thing the watch needs above all ends up causing its very demise.

Fascinating. Why are you telling me this?

You are such a rube. A beautifully made-up, dressed-up rube. You granted me full if inconvenient access to a practical tool listing the future in annoying increments.

And?

Well, I genuinely thought I was supposed to do something with them, running my grimy fingers on organically bonded edges.

Who told you? Did I tell you? Did anyone I sent tell you?

Not exactly. And that something my masters told me?

That was their business. I did not order or commission anyone to tell you anything.

Yes, the genuine, stubborn Masters of Suspicion. Shall I refresh your memory?

Jog it, as hard as you need to. You have my insipid permission.

Encounters with great men?

You ask enough of them, some are bound to answer.

The style flowing freely.

You may have exhibited a certain inclination, an ease. You are, however, the one who filled the frame with linotype. You wrote, oh, at least twenty pages.

Plus the notes.

Correct, plus the notes. The most delightful ones I have ever read. In a perfunctory way, naturally.

Or unnaturally. The way I created sounds became more impressive?

And a lot less significant. Your choice, randomly applied to a rather bulky, fricative table that, after all, belongs to everyone. I have no recollection of mailing you that compendium for Christmas.

Ha ha ha. And the story of parallel lives that can be imagined?

Oh! Now I should be held responsible for old pictures and archival repositories. And you claim that I am unfair and punishing. I am having a hard time following you. It is acceptable as I do not want to accompany you to the next condition.

What did I do?

Why did she come to me?

Why did she smile invisibly?

Why was her voice indexed on feline shapes?

What did I do?

Deafening, positively. Did when, to whom, and what about?

I ignored people. It was a learned trait, as you know. As an adult, it was mostly

Mostly after

After?

After that rather nasty day or have you already forgotten?

Must have.

The ruined one. If I understand anything to anything, you must have been there. You or someone looking exactly like you.

Oh that! I get it. Yes, I was a cannula. But I still don't follow you.

Am I being punished for that?

Oh, you mean, you think you are being chastised for the incident, shall we say? What a singular idea. What a crazy notion. You are not being punished for grammar, which after all is still your call, and rigorously awful. As you can imagine, we're not going to blame you for biology, not even biology gone awry.

It still has that feel, though. But then I will accept the assertion. So, what is it? No murder, no rape that I can remember. I never stole anything of any value.

Fine, fine. I must say that you are a lot less polished than you wish to appear. No wonder certain people would be fascinated, then repelled by you. So where were we?

I asked you a specific question.

Here is a specific answer: you did nothing.

Nothing?

Nothing.

So why the hard labor?

You call that hard? Think of your forebears. Think even of some of your friends. I could name a few.

Am I not being flogged? Everything new I ever fabricated became soiled. The writing I erased myself. Do you remember playing as a child with sympathetic ink?

Lemon juice.

You write. Nothing shows. You heat it, and all of a sudden you're a writer.

I have news for you: I invented the trick.

And I the reverse process. I do not blame it all on you. I just want to know how it came to pass.
What came to pass?
Her her her her her her her her her her
Yes her. Three letters, only one in its place.
Why do you not just order all my personal gaseous and hematic processes
To be discontinued
Even the fun ones?
Now, because I turn around and every time that flesh, smooth as a dolphin's skin, entirely sheathed in decency and subtlety and kindness and friendliness and charm and gentleness and sweetness and warmth and patience and brilliance and youth and loveliness and benevolence and solicitude and softness
All those words I just plain hate
I should not be able to spell or type them
In odium of every syllable, every character of them even in other words such as
Agraphia solstice and what butterflies call me
Well every time and forever it saturates my cheekbone, the same as in my parietal structure

Other of course than

Decomposed.

Is anyone listening?

Oh, I am letting you ramble on with much relish. But ask yourself this: what about what you are, were, and will be?

I am unsure and must refute. I can think of many despicable things I did at certain times. Telling stories. Yes, I told many stories. But being chastised for my paltry contribution to an entire narrative genre? It is not my fancy prose, is it? I cannot believe you pay that much attention to philology, prosody, minute scars. No, there has to be something else. What betrayal, what crime did I commit?

I wish I had skedaddled.

Instead, I paid the tribute, many times over, by staying, by going, by lying

Really? How ridiculous is that?

Can I be laid to rest with my industry at hand?

I will abide by every oath taken

I am different now

Better

Eternally imprecise. Better than what?

What I abhor the most: a weak prototype.

A Country like a Diseased Dance

I had given up, you know, quit.

And for no other reason than the test of time

The experience of having consummately shaped a festering obsession

One I can take to my grave without heavy lifting

And you, you, you, always hidden

You place another adder on my path

So slight as to be barely audible

So sumptuous as to cause me to refine the teleology of all this

So tenebrous I began to need her

You understand that I could have ceased to resist

Because

Because

Because

Because

Because I am one of those unable to recite that dedication

What?

You are not even this person for me

Merely a historical fact

A street urchin

What do I have to do with all this?

You know for a fact that if led, I will submit.

So I beg of you tear off my wings

Or I will, first with the most.

You comprehend.

Do you think I feel threatened?

I only wish to be left alone.

Who ever is?

She will not speak to me and yet her timber of amethysts follows my every neuronal impulse.

Even in the gap?

Especially there. That is where her image hangs.

Sheesh. I had no clue we were making it so hard for you. I am beginning to feel sorry. You really want me to turn off the light?

I beseech you (a word far superior to any other way of asking)

Answer

Answer

Are you the one crying now?

So you do recall. Tell you what. The last one is on me. Then you go. How does that grab you? I must talk to my superior but that is practically a formality. I am starting to understand what I did to you.

Would it be presumptuous to ask for her happiness too?

Yes, but today I cannot refuse you anything.

Answers, you said answers.

And that is one. Your last sip of coffee is the key to it all. What do you sense?

Cortical numbness. A thousand million illuminations dreading lack of data. It is working.

You should see the smile on your face. I am sincerely sorry.

Do not be. I am not. The memory is now empty

About the Author

Born nowhere in particular twenty years after the most significant event of his life, Larry Benjamin was raised in France. A graduate of Portland State University and Brown University, he has had several careers, from college professor to entrepreneur and back to educator. He has also been writing what may be poetry for the past twenty years. He now resides in the Deep South, not very far from nowhere in particular, with his wife, Mary, and two delinquent cats, Dexie and Ezra (the Scribe). He is a watch collector and a student of the first sword-style codified in Japan, Tenshin Shōden Katori Shintō-ryū.

www.ingramcontent.com/pod-product-compliance
Lightning Source LLC
Chambersburg PA
CBHW060533080526
44586CB00012B/718